STRESS LESS **COLOR-BY-NUMBER**™
MANDALAS
75 COLORING PAGES FOR PEACE AND RELAXATION

Adams Media
New York London Toronto Sydney New Delhi

Adamsmedia

Adams Media
An Imprint of Simon & Schuster, Inc.
100 Technology Center Drive
Stoughton, MA 02072

For information about special discounts for bulk purchases, please contact Simon & Schuster Special Sales at 1-866-506-1949 or business@simonandschuster.com.

The Simon & Schuster Speakers Bureau can bring authors to your live event. For more information or to book an event contact the Simon & Schuster Speakers Bureau at 1-866-248-3049 or visit our website at www.simonspeakers.com.

Manufactured in the United States of America

2 2021

Library of Congress Cataloging-in-Publication Data has been applied for.

ISBN 978-1-5072-0127-5

This book is intended as general information only, and should not be used to diagnose or treat any health condition. In light of the complex, individual, and specific nature of health problems, this book is not intended to replace professional medical advice. The ideas, procedures, and suggestions in this book are intended to supplement, not replace, the advice of a trained medical professional. Consult your physician before adopting any of the suggestions in this book, as well as about any condition that may require diagnosis or medical attention. The author and publisher disclaim any liability arising directly or indirectly from the use of this book.

Contains material adapted from the following title *The Big Book of Mandalas Coloring Book, Volume 2*,
copyright © 2015 by Simon & Schuster, Inc., ISBN 978-1-4405-8625-5.

INTRODUCTION

Looking to relax? Searching for a connection with both the world around you and your own subconscious needs and desires? If you're looking to get rid of all the extra stress in your life, just pick up a pencil, crayon, or marker and let *Stress Less Color-By-Number™ Mandalas* help you manage your worries in an easy, meditative way.

Coloring in the 75 mandalas (Sanskrit for *circle*) throughout this book will help you increase your creativity, relieve stress, and find a sense of balance in your life. This soothing act is easy to do and doesn't pressure you to problem-solve, leaving your mind free to focus on the mandala and any thoughts that the calming, repetitive nature of coloring the circle brings to mind.

Each mandala has been numbered so you can achieve beautiful results without the worry of choosing the colors yourself. Refer to the insert's color palette to find the color that corresponds with each number. Any spaces that aren't numbered should remain white. You'll also find a fully colored version of each mandala on the insert pages to give you a preview of the beautiful picture you will create when you follow the number pattern exactly. But if you'd rather, let your own unique palette guide your hand and personalize your image. Whichever color you feel like using is the right choice.

So whether you're new to mandalas or have been embracing their meditative qualities for years, it's time to stress less and open your mind, take a deep meditative breath and step into the circle.

MANDALA 1

MANDALA 2

MANDALA 3

MANDALA 4

MANDALA 5

MANDALA 6

MANDALA 7

MANDALA 8

MANDALA 9

MANDALA 10

MANDALA 11

MANDALA 12

MANDALA 13

MANDALA 14

MANDALA 15

MANDALA 16

MANDALA 17

MANDALA 18

MANDALA 19

MANDALA 20

MANDALA 21

MANDALA 22

MANDALA 23

MANDALA 24

MANDALA 25

MANDALA 26

MANDALA 27

MANDALA 28

MANDALA 29

MANDALA 30

MANDALA 31

MANDALA 32

MANDALA 33

MANDALA 34

MANDALA 35

MANDALA 36

MANDALA 37

MANDALA 38

MANDALA 39

MANDALA 40

MANDALA 41

MANDALA 42

MANDALA 43

MANDALA 44

MANDALA 45

MANDALA 46

MANDALA 47

MANDALA 48

MANDALA 49

MANDALA 50

MANDALA 51

MANDALA 52

MANDALA 53

MANDALA 54

MANDALA 55

MANDALA 56

MANDALA 57

MANDALA 58

MANDALA 60

MANDALA 61

MANDALA 62

MANDALA 63

MANDALA 64

MANDALA 65

MANDALA 66

MANDALA 67

MANDALA 68

MANDALA 69

MANDALA 70

MANDALA 71

MANDALA 72

MANDALA 73

MANDALA 74

MANDALA 75

TEST PAGES

COLORED MANDALA
REFERENCE GUIDE

COLOR KEY

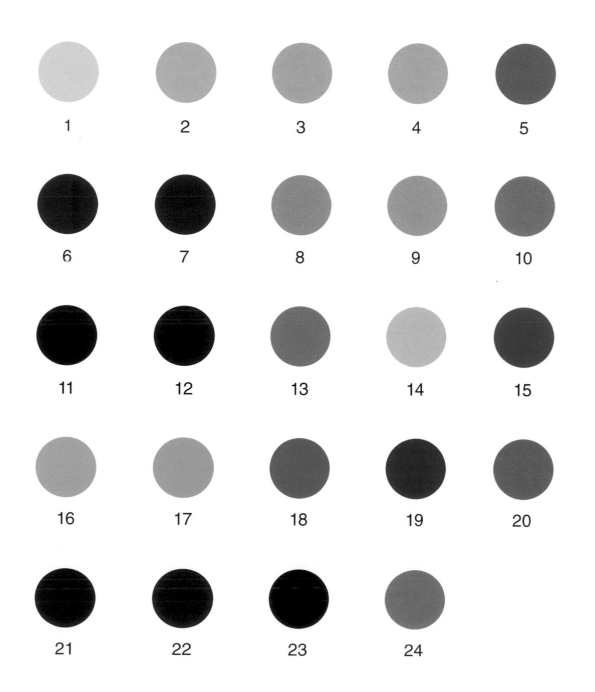

1

2

3

5

6

4

7

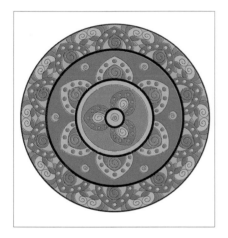

8

9

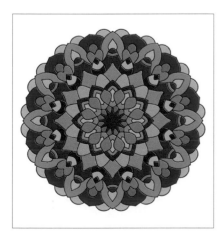

10

11

12

13   14   15

16   17   18

19

20

21

22

23

24

25　　　　　　　　26　　　　　　　　27

29

28　　　　　　　　30

31

32

33

34

35

36

37

38

39

41

40

42

43

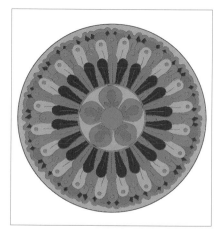

44

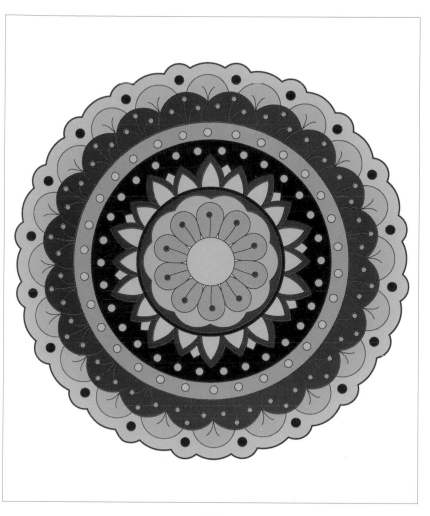

45

46

47

48

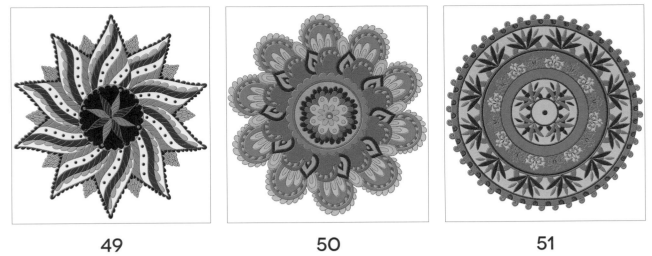

49 50 51

52

53

54

55

57

56

58

59

60

61

62

63

65

64

66

67

68

69

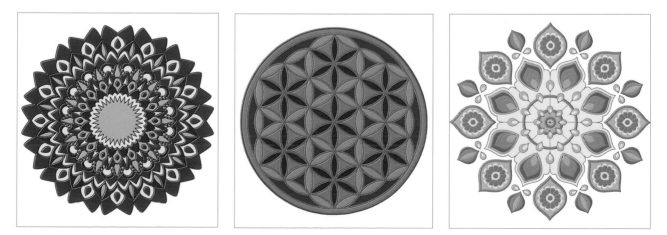

70

71

72

73

74

75